VICTORY 1918
THE LAST 100 DAYS

TIM COOK AND J. L. GRANATSTEIN

CANADIAN WAR MUSEUM
MUSÉE CANADIEN DE LA GUERRE

Library and Archives Canada
Cataloguing in Publication

Cook, Tim, author
Victory 1918: the last 100 days /
Tim Cook and J. L. Granatstein.

(Souvenir catalogue series,
ISSN 2291-6385; 24)
Issued also in French under title:
Victoire 1918.
ISBN 978-0-660-25254-4 (softcover)
Cat. no.: NM23-5/24-2018E

1. Canada. Canadian Army. Canadian
    Corps – History – Exhibitions.
2. World War, 1914-1918 – Campaigns –
    Western Front – Exhibitions.
3. World War, 1914-1918 – Canada –
    Exhibitions.
I. Granatstein, J. L., author.

II. Canadian War Museum, issuing body.
III. Title.
IV. Series: Souvenir catalogue series; 24.

D547.C2C5555 2018
940.4'1271
C2018-904992-8

Published by the
Canadian War Museum
1 Vimy Place
Ottawa, ON K1A 0M8
warmuseum.ca

Printed and bound in Canada

Graphic design and cover by:
ninesixteen Creative Inc.

Souvenir Catalogue series, 24
ISSN 2291-6385

CONTENTS

FOREWORD

The First World War was won in the last hundred days. In a series of bitterly fought battles along the Western Front between August and November 1918, seasoned Canadian soldiers played a critical role in defeating the Germans and securing a final peace.

The Hundred Days campaign was a different kind of war. Unlike earlier in the war, when the front lines were in a stalemate much of time, the campaign was characterized by significant gains made in rapid succession. Gone was the inertia of mud-soaked trench warfare that had dominated soldiers' lives for the past four years.

And yet there were no bloodless victories. The critical role the Canadian Corps played in these battles came at a terrible cost, with more than 45,000 casualties between the initial offensive at Amiens and the final struggle at Mons. Led by the enduring figure of Sir Arthur Currie, Canadian "shock troops" contributed significantly to the Allied victory. The enemy forces were defeated, and occupied French and Belgium civilians were liberated.

To mark the centenary of the Hundred Days campaign, the Canadian War Museum presents **Victory 1918 – The Last 100 Days**. The exhibition and this catalogue help illuminate these final, decisive days, at once unimaginably dark and filled with hope.

Using the words and images of combatants and non-combatants, the exhibition captures the small moments of endurance and courage, along with titanic battles and great victories. It explores the human cost paid by Canadians in combat.

Battle by battle, from Amiens through Arras to Cambrai and finally at Mons, Canadian troops overcame fearsome German defences with dedicated preparation, unimaginable bravery and innovative tactics.

The comprehensive Allied victory was secured with Canadian leadership, training, logistics, technology — and lives.

A hundred years on, the men and women who had first-hand memory of the Great War have all passed away and it is up to us to remember their sacrifice. This exhibition honours their efforts, their fears, and most of all, their fight for peace.

James Whitham
Acting Director General
Canadian War Museum

INTRODUCTION

The Hundred Days campaign was the most important series of battles fought by the Canadian Corps in the First World War. Yet most Canadians have never heard of Amiens, the Drocourt-Quéant Line, the Canal du Nord, Cambrai or Valenciennes.

Generations of Canadians have focused instead on commemorating Vimy, the key battle of the Canadian Corps in April 1917. The Battle of Vimy Ridge was more important for its effect on morale than for its strategic consequences.

And while the Canadians took a key German position, it did not change the course of the war — the conflict continued for another 19 months. The Hundred Days campaign, in contrast, was a signal event that forever marked the four divisions of the Corps as elite "shock troops."

In massive offensives starting in March 1918, the Germans had hurled themselves at the Allies. While they failed to drive the British and French from the war, both sides suffered heavily, with the Germans losing some 800,000 soldiers. The Allies lost even more but could better absorb the casualties, especially when the Americans began to arrive in strength at the Western Front. The time was ripe for a counterattack.

Coordinated by supreme commander Marshal Ferdinand Foch, the Allied armies began a series of assaults on the Germans in July. When these met with success, the Canadians were ordered into action as part of the larger offensive. The Hundred Days campaign would begin on August 8, 1918, east of Amiens.

The Canadian Corps was a battle-tested formation. It had proven itself in 1917: at Vimy in April, at Hill 70 in August and at Passchendaele in October and November. The Corps was led by Lieutenant-General Sir Arthur Currie, who had taken command in June of that year. The Canadians had been training since May 1918 and were ready for battle: the infantry, tanks, artillery and other combat arms working together to better smash the enemy defences.

The Corps' infantry battalions were larger than the British: the Canadians had extra artillery and machine guns, additional trucks, and more engineers.

But the Germans knew that the Canadian presence heralded an attack. And so the Corps moved to the front — in secret — under a "Keep your mouth shut!" order aimed at stifling loose talk among soldiers. The logistical challenge of transporting 100,000 soldiers, more than 20,000 horses, equipment, weapons, supplies, ammunition and food equated to moving a large Canadian city 63 kilometres. That it was done secretly made the achievement even more impressive.

Flanked by Australian, French and British troops, the Canadian assault at Amiens was launched at 4:20 a.m. on August 8. The enemy staggered under the artillery barrage, a mass tank attack, hundreds of Royal Air Force fighters and bombers overhead — combined arms warfare with the Canadian infantry in the lead. When the Germans fell back, their casualties heavy, the Allies advanced 13 kilometres: a significant gain in a war marked so far by small, costly advances.

But the Germans were not finished. They rushed in reinforcements, slowing the advance as the Canadians' supply lines lengthened and their wounded mounted. When gains in driving the Germans back slowed over several days, Currie, supported by the Australian Corps commander, asked his British superiors to end the battle so that the Canadians could launch future offensives. The Amiens offensive had resulted in more than 9,000 Germans captured, countless killed, nearly 200 guns taken and 27 French villages liberated.

Before Amiens, the Allied high command had assumed the war would extend into 1919, and possibly 1920. This battle shocked both sides. Was German morale crumbling? Could the war end sooner?

The Allies planned a series of late August assaults, and the Canadian Corps would spearhead another attack.

The Corps' objective was the German defences east of Arras. These included the feared Drocourt-Quéant Line — an anchor fortification along the 10-kilometre-deep system protected by trenches, rows of barbed wire, and concrete bunkers packed with machine guns and resolute troops.

At 3 a.m. on August 26, behind a hurricane of artillery fire, the Corps advanced. The enemy retaliated, fiercely and relentlessly. On the first day, the Canadians advanced 5 kilometres. The next two days, they managed an additional 3 kilometres in intense combat: they attacked, dug in, battled the German counterattacks and advanced again.

They defeated several enemy divisions, took 3,300 prisoners and captured 519 machine guns, but suffered 5,801 casualties in three days. Currie ordered a pause to regroup, calling this "the hardest fighting" in the Corps' history.

The Canadians still faced the heavily defended Drocourt-Quéant Line. After days of raids and artillery fire, they struck on September 2. The Germans fought doggedly but their forces were smashed, with over 6,000 prisoners taken and almost 500 machine guns seized. Another 5,622 Canadians were killed or wounded, taking the total losses to over 11,000.

The German high command ordered a retirement eastward to new positions behind the Canal du Nord, which ran north to south and formed a significant barrier. On the eastern side of the canal, in fortified trenches, the Germans were determined to defend Cambrai. As their key supply centre in northern France, its loss would be catastrophic.

The battered Canadians, having achieved two significant victories at the cost of almost 25,000 casualties, now faced the challenge of crossing the canal. Currie decided to concentrate his forces in front of a dry stretch of the waterway, with lead units surging across at zero hour and fanning out on the other side.

Behind these advancing troops, engineers would then build bridges to get guns, trucks and follow-on infantry across. But there were risks. If the enemy caught sight of the concentrated troops, they would be slaughtered. His British superiors thought the plan risky, but Currie persisted, confident in his soldiers.

The September 27 assault toward Cambrai went as planned: the infantry crossed the canal quickly and the engineers immediately threw bridges over, despite facing shellfire. Although driven back, the Germans fought zealously, hurling fresh divisions into battle. Bitter fighting continued for 11 days, with the enemy contesting every metre of ground and counterattacking repeatedly. But in the early hours of October 9, the Canadians took the city.

Their engineers moved in to douse the fires the retreating Germans had set in the hope of razing the crucial logistical centre. Capturing Cambrai came at a high cost in lives, but it destabilized the entire German front in northern France. Since the Arras battle, elements of 31 German divisions had been defeated by the Canadian Corps.

The Great War was now in its final phase. The enemy soldiers pulled back and used delaying tactics to slow the Allied advance, with many costly firefights and skirmishes. A last major artillery battle and infantry assault at Valenciennes on November 1 brought another Canadian victory and further German retreat. By the night of November 10, Canadian troops were at Mons, the symbolic city where the British had begun their retreat in August 1914.

The Canadians captured Mons by dawn on the 11th, when word came of an Armistice at 11 o'clock that day. The Canadian Corps had played a vital role in the campaign, contributing far more than any other corps on the Western Front. Victories at Amiens, Arras, Cambrai and Valenciennes were key to breaking the enemy's prepared defences.

But the cost was terrible. During the Hundred Days campaign, the Canadians suffered over 45,000 killed, wounded and taken prisoner, which amounted to almost one-fifth of the total Canadian casualties in four years of war.

The war from 1914 to August 1918 had seen millions of casualties without measurable gain. The victories of the Hundred Days defeated the German Army in the field and brought the First World War to an end.

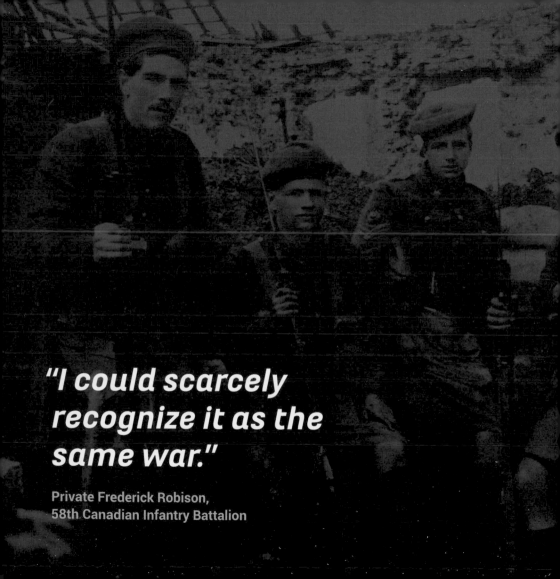

"I could scarcely recognize it as the same war."

Private Frederick Robison,
58th Canadian Infantry Battalion

PREPARING FOR BATTLE

THE HUNDRED DAYS — AUGUST 8 TO NOVEMBER 11, 1918

The Hundred Days campaign was a series of great battles in late 1918 that defeated the German Army and ended the First World War.

The Canadian Corps spearheaded many of these assaults. Its combined arms — infantry, tanks, artillery and aircraft — worked together to break the stalemate of the trenches.

THE CORPS

Led by Lieutenant-General Sir Arthur Currie and made up of four infantry divisions, the Canadian Corps was a battle-hardened formation.

Although the Corps fought as part of the British Expeditionary Force, Currie, as a national commander, had some flexibility to demand more guns, engineers and trucks than any British corps. The Corps' 100,000 soldiers almost always fought together. By 1918, the Corps had become the shock troops of the British forces.

More than 620,000 Canadians enlisted during the war and 425,000 were sent overseas. Almost all were civilians, coming from farms and factories across the country.

A typical recruit was 26 years old, had a grade six education and had worked as a labourer. Only men could enlist to fight. About 3,000 Canadian women served as military nurses.

THE COMMANDER

Lieutenant-General Sir Arthur Currie was Canada's greatest battlefield commander. A real-estate developer and militia officer before the war, Currie commanded a brigade and then a division before leading the Canadian Corps from June 1917 onward.

Currie was a careful general. He studied the battlefield, planned methodically, listened to his staff officers and tried to minimize the Corps' casualties while maximizing the enemy's.

Currie was a big man. He was almost 2 metres tall and weighed over 110 kilograms. On his wool service dress jacket, the shoulder straps indicate the rank of lieutenant-general.

**Lieutenant-General
Currie's Uniform**

TRAINING FOR OPEN WARFARE

Learning from earlier German and Allied tactical errors, Currie ordered his soldiers to train hard in the summer of 1918.

Soldiers had to use initiative and keep moving after meeting each objective. The tempo of battle quickened, with attacks planned and executed rapidly to surprise the enemy. Infantry companies and battalions learned to cooperate with artillery, tanks and aircraft, mastering the new tactics of combined arms warfare.

> *"Never has our training been more severe; every day makes it clearer that when we move it will be to enter the bloodiest fight in which we have yet taken part."*
>
> Sergeant L. McLeod Gould, 102nd Canadian Infantry Battalion

ARMY FORM W.3066.

To be pasted in A.B. 439 and A.B. 64.

KEEP YOUR MOUTH SHUT!

The success of any operation we carry out depends chiefly on surprise.

DO NOT TALK.—When you know that your Unit is making preparations for an attack, don't talk about them to men in other Units or to strangers, and keep your mouth shut, especially in public places.

Do not be inquisitive about what other Units are doing; if you hear or see anything, keep it to yourself.

If you hear anyone else talking about operations, stop him at once.

The success of the operations and the lives of your comrades depend upon your SILENCE.

If you ever should have the misfortune to be taken prisoner, don't give the enemy any information beyond your rank and name. In answer to all other questions you need only say, "I cannot answer."

He cannot compel you to give any other information. He may use threats. He will respect you if your courage, patriotism, and self-control do not fail. Every word you say may cause the death of one of your comrades.

Either after or before you are openly examined, Germans, disguised as British Officers or men, will be sent among you or will await you in the cages or quarters or hospital to which you are taken.

Germans will be placed where they can overhear what you say without being seen by you.

DO NOT BE TAKEN IN BY ANY OF THESE TRICKS.

Pt. in France by A.P. & S.S.   Press C. X477. 500000. 7/18.

SECRET OPERATION

After a number of offensives beginning in March 1918, the German Army was tremendously weakened, suffering over 800,000 casualties. The Allies made plans to counterattack.

The new Allied commander, Marshal Ferdinand Foch, ordered a series of offensives. French and American soldiers attacked at the Marne River in July 1918 and the British planned to strike east of the city of Amiens in August 1918. Canadian and Australian infantry formations would spearhead the drive, while British and French forces assisted with tanks, air power, infantry and artillery.

The planned strike to the east of Amiens was to be a surprise operation. With all soldiers known to talk freely and speculate about upcoming offensives, each Canadian soldier had this "Keep Your Mouth Shut!" order posted into his pay book.

Gunner Phillip Henry Button's Pay Book

"You had the feeling that everything was well planned, well organized.... Everything seemed to go like clockwork."

Lieutenant G.S. Rutherford, 52nd Canadian Infantry Battalion

PLANNING THE BATTLE

A successful attack involved putting vast quantities of weapons, ammunition and men, along with other supplies, in place — without raising the Germans' suspicions. The entire Canadian Corps, over 100,000 soldiers and 20,000 horses, was secretly moved south from the Arras area to Amiens.

Warm food, tea and rum were essential for keeping up soldiers' morale. This portable pack allowed food to be carried to the soldiers as they waited in the front lines.

Insulated Food Container ➤

BEFORE THE BATTLE

Nervous soldiers waited in silence before the battle. In a few hours they might be killed or wounded. Officers issued strong rum to calm nerves. Watches were synchronized and set for the zero hour — 4:20 a.m.

Private Charles John Cook of the 19th Canadian Infantry Battalion used this official army watch, recognizable as such by its Broad Arrow mark, during the battle. Cook was holding the watch three weeks later on August 27, when he was severely wounded in an attack at Monchy, east of Arras.

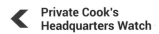

Private Cook's Headquarters Watch

"We shot them down like dogs. We kept going and came to their support lines where we killed some more."

Corporal Deward Barnes,
19th Canadian Infantry Battalion

AMIENS

SHOCK AND AWE –
AUGUST 8, 1918

The Allied attack began at 4:20 a.m. with the massed guns firing a heavy barrage. Tanks crushed the barbed wire and knocked out enemy machine guns, while the infantry moved quickly, keeping pace with the barrage of shells and advancing 60 metres every two minutes.

After the initial shock to the enemy, intense combat continued along the front. Canadian soldiers thrust 13 kilometres into enemy lines, driving the Germans steadily back. It appeared that the Allies might break through the German trench system and into the open fields beyond.

The success of the Allied assault on August 8 shocked the Germans, who suffered some 27,000 killed, wounded and captured. But the cost was high on all sides: Canadian casualties on that day were 1,036 killed and 2,803 wounded.

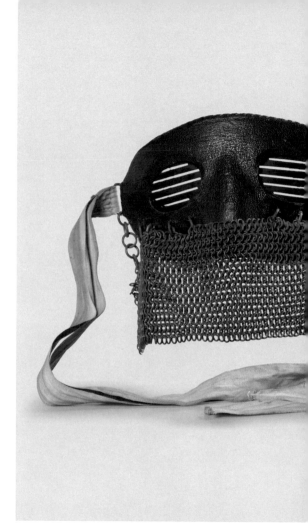

AN ARMOURED THRUST

The Allies grouped 604 tanks for the surprise attack. Tanks moved slowly but inspired fear in the enemy as they overran barbed wire and provided supporting fire for advancing infantry. Their impact on August 8 was significant. But rough terrain, mechanical failure and enemy fire knocked most of them out. The tanks proved far less effective in the second and third days of battle.

Leather helmets with face masks like this one offered the crew some protection. While the tanks were bulletproof, armour-piercing rounds or high explosives could penetrate the machine's steel hull. Another danger was "splash": metal fragments sent flying through the crew compartment by the force of shells or other projectiles hitting the steel hull.

Anti-Splinter Face Mask

**Mauser Tankgewehr
M1918 Anti-Tank Rifle**

ANTI-TANK RIFLE

This single-shot bolt-action German anti-tank rifle fired a high-velocity 13.2-mm armour-piercing round. The rifle was fired from a static position and had an effective range of about 500 metres, but it had a punishing recoil that bruised shoulders. It took enormous bravery for an infantryman to face off against a tank.

Although the Allied tanks contributed to the victory at Amiens, they were rapidly knocked out by enemy fire or mechanical failure. By August 11, only 38 of the 343 Mark Vs that started the battle were in running order. Tanks were not a war-winning weapon.

TWO HEROES

The advancing Canadians faced small-arms fire and shell blasts, finding ways to keep moving even as their comrades fell. In a remarkable act of bravery, two Canadians from the 13th Canadian Infantry Battalion rushed the enemy to clear the way for the advance — both received the Victoria Cross for their actions. One lived and one died.

Corporal Herman Good from South Bathurst, New Brunswick, charged three German machine guns. Attacking the position alone, he survived the crossfire of bullets, killing the gunners or forcing them to surrender. Later, he led another frontal assault against a battery of enemy 5.9-inch guns, knocking out their crew.

For his uncommon bravery, Good was awarded the Victoria Cross. Promoted to sergeant, he survived the war.

Private John Bernard Croak of Little Bay, Newfoundland, single-handedly knocked out a machine gun during the advance. Although severely wounded, he refused medical aid and led his platoon in a second bold attack on an enemy strongpoint of three machine guns. Croak suffered mortal wounds and died minutes later. For his bravery in the assault, he was posthumously awarded the Victoria Cross.

 Corporal Good's Medal Set

1. Victoria Cross
2. British War Medal 1914–1920
3. Victory Medal 1914–1919
4. King George VI Coronation Medal, 1937
5. Queen Elizabeth II Coronation Medal, 1953
6. Canadian Centennial Medal, 1967

 Corporal Good

HENRY BYCE

Born in Westmeath, Ontario, Sergeant Henry Byce was awarded the Distinguished Conduct Medal for his actions on the night of August 8. Despite being wounded in the neck and shoulder, Byce led an attack on several machine guns that opened the way for a deeper thrust into enemy lines.

The Distinguished Conduct Medal is the second-highest gallantry award for non-commissioned soldiers after the Victoria Cross. Byce also received the Médaille militaire, France's second-highest medal for gallantry. He was one of only 55 Canadians honoured with the award. Byce survived the war, returning to Chapleau, Ontario.

 Sergeant Byce's Medal Set

1. Distinguished Conduct Medal
2. British War Medal 1914–1920
3. Victory Medal 1914–1919
4. War Medal 1939–1945
5. Médaille militaire (France)

BREAKDOWN IN COMMUNICATION

Communication between advancing infantry and commanders in the rear relied on a fragile network. Aircraft provided key information from the sky and the infantry also passed messages by telephone, signal flags, pigeons and runners. But heavy shellfire often cut wires and killed runners, while flags and signals were obscured by the smoke and dust.

This British-made field telephone set was used to communicate by voice and Morse code from the front lines to the rear. The leather satchel is inscribed 53rd BTY; 310813 CROULSTON, indicating that it was used by Driver George Croulston of the Canadian Field Artillery, who was injured in the Hundred Days campaign.

Telephone Set, D Mk. 1

LOGISTICS

The Allied advance slowed on August 9. The surprise was over. With the extent of the Canadian advance, tens of thousands of shells and artillery pieces had to be pulled or driven forward to catch up to the infantry, who were running short of supplies. Often they were slow to arrive and attacks were delayed.

Enemy reinforcements were hurled into the line and the Canadian infantry battled them in fierce combat. While the Canadians continued to drive the Germans back, both sides suffered heavy casualties. Canadian Corps commander Sir Arthur Currie wrote by August 9 that "the enemy's resistance stiffened considerably, and whatever gains were made

resulted from heavy Infantry fighting against fresh troops, with only a few tanks available for support." On August 11, six new German divisions, along with several batteries of artillery, were thrown into battle. Each assault came at a higher cost with fewer gains. There would be no breakthrough.

"The bodies of men and horses were strewn all about, mangled in every possible manner."

Private C. J. Cate,
12th Battery, Canadian Field Artillery

AFTERMATH

The Germans suffered a major defeat at Amiens.

The Canadian Corps battered 15 enemy divisions and captured 9,311 prisoners. The Allies had broken through the German trench lines, but logistical restraints and a determined enemy ensured that they could not yet make it further into open country.

This warfare was far different from the grinding trench battles earlier in the war, but there were no easy victories on the Western Front. The Canadian Corps suffered 11,822 casualties at Amiens.

MEMORIAL CROSS

This Memorial Cross was issued to Private Francis Charles Heath's family after he was killed in battle on August 9, 1918. Heath was a farmer who enlisted at Lacombe, Alberta.

The Memorial Cross, or Silver Cross, was issued to the mothers and widows of Canadian military personnel who died during the war. It is presented to this day.

Private Heath's Memorial Cross

"I could never quite understand how anyone survived at all in an attack of this kind."

Sergeant Arthur Shelford,
54th Canadian Infantry Battalion

ARRAS

THE ASSAULT AT ARRAS

The Canadian Corps moved north from its hard-fought victory at Amiens to the Arras front, east of Vimy Ridge.

Only days after the Battle of Amiens, Lieutenant-General Sir Arthur Currie's soldiers prepared for a frontal assault against one of the German Army's most powerful defence systems. Fortified over the years, it relied on multiple machine-gun teams defending the front in protected concrete pillboxes. In places along the front, the barbed wire lay 75 metres deep.

Only with concentrated shellfire could the Allies destroy enough of it to allow their infantry to pass. From August 26 to September 2, 1918, all four Canadian divisions, aided by British troops and artillery, smashed the enemy positions. This was a brutal battle.

HARD FIGHTING — AUGUST 26 TO 28, 1918

At 3 a.m. on August 26, Canadian infantry attacked behind a creeping barrage of shellfire. There was no breakthrough, only slow, grinding and costly warfare as the Canadians clawed their way forward. Desperate to hold the front, the Germans rushed reinforcements forward and counterattacked repeatedly.

On August 28, a day of limited gains and fierce resistance from the Germans, Currie ordered a pause in the fighting to regroup and plan a new assault.

REBUILDING THE CORPS

>

Top:
Silver Coin

Bottom:
Locket

In 1918, close to 100,000 young men would be conscripted in Canada for service overseas, with some 24,000 arriving at the front by November 1918. These reinforcements were essential in bringing the infantry battalions up to strength after each battle. Conscripts were initially viewed with suspicion by the enlisted men, but most soon found themselves integrated into their units through the forge of fire.

These mementos belonged to Earl McDermid, with the photograph in the locket showing him and his wife Margaret Wilson. Private McDermid, a school teacher from Nottawasaga Township in Simcoe County, was a conscript who served with the 18th Canadian Infantry Battalion. The 34-year-old infantryman arrived at the front on August 20 and fought through the remaining battles of the Hundred Days campaign.

INFANTRY ATTACK

The battle against the German trench system, known as the Hindenburg Line, saw waves of Canadian infantry attacking behind a barrage of artillery shells. Riflemen and machine gunners fired at the enemy soldiers to force them to take cover, while other Canadians threw or launched grenades to clear out the defences. But the Germans were prepared and determined. Their positions were anchored around machine-gun posts and they often fought from concrete pillboxes. The battle raged back and forth for three days.

Pulling the ring on this "Mills Bomb" No. 5 grenade gave the soldier four seconds to throw it. Its explosion sent shards of metal in all directions: it was a key weapon in destroying enemy strongpoints.

No. 5 Grenade

GEORGES VANIER

Major Georges Philéas Vanier served with the 22nd Canadian Infantry Battalion, the only infantry unit that was all French Canadian. At Arras, he led the battalion when the commanding officer was wounded. After two days of bitter fighting, the unit had suffered crippling casualties but Vanier led a final assault against German positions near the village of Chérisy on August 28. Badly wounded by a shell, his right leg had to be amputated.

This watercolour depicts the 22nd Battalion's Chérisy attack on August 28. Major Georges Vanier is believed to be the officer in the centre, leading his men forward against strong enemy resistance. Throughout the fighting at Arras, the battalion suffered 435 casualties. Vanier himself was badly wounded.

Over the Top

Painted by Alfred Bastien in 1918

German
Machine Gun,
MG-08

"The Hun seemed to be depending upon the large number of his machine guns rather than his artillery to hold us back."

Lieutenant Ivan Maharg,
1st Canadian Mounted Rifles

GERMAN PILLBOXES

The German defences throughout the Arras trench system were anchored by hundreds of pillboxes and machine-gun posts. With concrete walls and roofs up to one-third of a metre thick, these dugouts were almost immune to shellfire.

The Germans relied heavily on their elite machine gunners to defend a sector or trench. The MG-08 heavy machine gun fired up to 500 bullets a minute. It was a deadly weapon that, when used in combination with other machine guns to create overlapping zones of fire, could mow down any soldier in its path.

COSTLY BATTLES

To advance forward, the Canadians had to destroy each pillbox and machine gun. Success depended on innovative tactics, and soldiers with extraordinary courage and a willingness to sacrifice their lives in battle.

From August 26 to 28, two Canadian divisions fought eight kilometres into the enemy trenches in some of the most difficult battles of the war. The Canadian divisions suffered 5,801 casualties, while the Germans lost more, including 3,300 prisoners. Attesting to the strength of the German defences, a staggering 519 machine guns were captured. On August 28, Currie ordered a pause to allow new, fresh divisions to rotate to the front for another assault.

A German Pill-Box After an Attack

Painted by William Topham between 1916 and 1918

THE DANGEROUS ACT OF SURRENDER

The process of surrender was always dangerous. In the heat of battle, soldiers were frustrated, scared — and vengeful. Canadian soldiers' eyewitness accounts reveal that German soldiers trying to surrender were sometimes executed on the battlefield. It was more often the fate of snipers or machine gunners who had fired to the last bullet and then expected mercy.

Unlawful killings were committed by soldiers in all armies. Despite this, at Arras most Germans survived the process of surrender, with the Canadians capturing more than 10,000 prisoners.

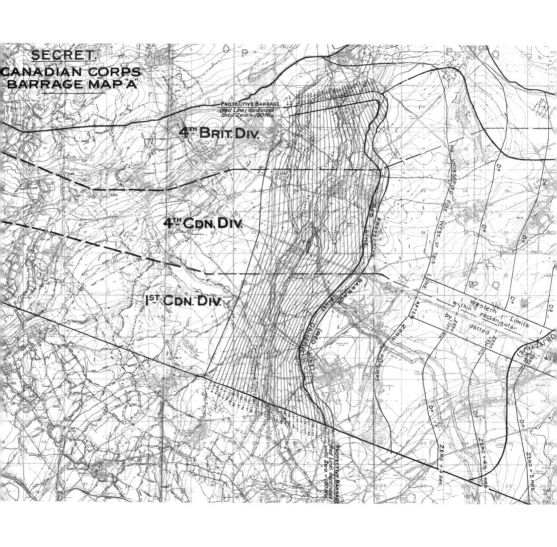

BREAKING THE DROCOURT-QUÉANT LINE — SEPTEMBER 2, 1918

The Germans were desperate to hold their trenches along the Arras front, and they sent thousands of reinforcements, machine-gun units and artillery batteries to defend them.

After a pause to regroup, the Canadians attacked again on September 2 behind a hurricane of shells. Tremendous tactical skill, courage and grit carried the Canadian infantry forward as they swarmed over the enemy positions. By the end of the day, the German forces were broken, fleeing southeast to their Canal du Nord position.

This complex barrage map was used by the Canadian and British soldiers manning the 559 field guns and heavy howitzers that supported the Canadian attack on September 2.

Each line on the map indicates a forward lift of the carefully timed creeping barrage of shells that the infantry followed during the advance.

CARING FOR THE WOUNDED

The Canadian Army Medical Corps developed a complex and effective system to treat wounded and ill soldiers.

The "walking wounded" who stumbled off the battlefield, and the more seriously injured who were carried by stretcher-bearer teams, received initial treatment at the Regimental Aid Post.

The key to survival was rapid evacuation — through the chain of field ambulances and aid stations — to more effective medical assistance and surgery further to the rear.

While many soldiers died before they reached medical care, the system ensured that only 11.6 per cent of the wounded and less than 1 per cent of the sick died.

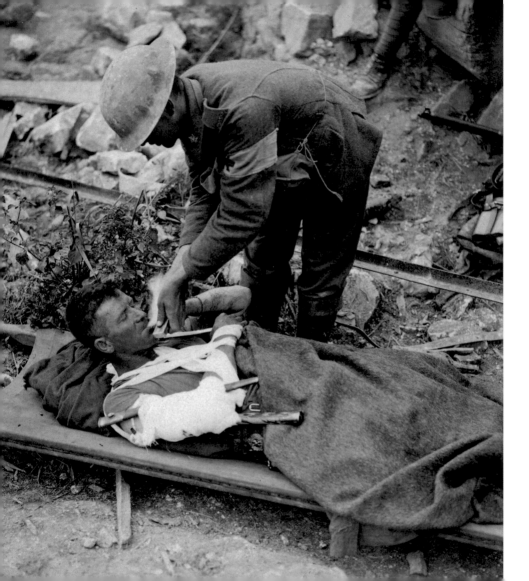

FIELD SURGICAL KIT

Knives, clamps, razors and all manner of tools were available to the field surgeon, who had to cut open uniforms and flesh to extract metal, dirt and clothing. Leaving foreign objects in wounds almost always led to fatal infections, in the age before antibiotics.

NEW BLOOD

Blood transfusion was in its infancy during the war, but several Canadian medical officers were innovators in the art. Soldiers who survived their initial wounds often died from shock and loss of blood. Blood was drawn directly from the donor and transfused through tubing to the patient in need.

"I have no doubt whatsoever that the transfusion saved my life."

**Major Georges Vanier,
22nd Canadian Infantry Battalion**

Top: Field Surgical Kit
Bottom: Blood Transfusion Kit

LILLIAN GALBRAITH

Nursing Sister Lillian Ellen Galbraith from Barrie, Ontario, was a pre-war nurse who served in a number of hospitals and medical units in Salonika, Malta and Britain. Galbraith was one of almost 3,000 Nursing Sisters who cared for the wounded during the war. For her long service from 1915 to 1920, she was awarded the Royal Red Cross, Class 2 medal.

 Nursing Sister Galbraith's Medal Set

1. Royal Red Cross, Class 2 (ARRC)
2. 1914–1915 Star
3. British War Medal 1914–1920
4. Victory Medal 1914–1919

A COSTLY VICTORY

The Canadian Corps smashed through one of the toughest German positions on the Western Front and sent the enemy fleeing eastward behind the Canal du Nord. Currie described the Canadians' breaking of the German defences at Arras as "the hardest battle in its history."

The Canadians met and defeated seven German divisions and captured thousands of prisoners. The cost was witheringly high, with over 5,500 Canadian casualties from September 1 to 2, and 11,423 recorded Canadian casualties for the entire battle.

This temporary grave marker was erected by the 16th Canadian Infantry Battalion in memory of some of the officers and men killed in action in the attack on September 2, who were likely buried in a mass grave.

The German forces had been soundly beaten again, but there was more fighting to come.

Grave Marker

"It is truly impossible for me to find words to adequately express the truly wonderful fighting qualities our men displayed ... a lump comes in one's throat whenever you think about it."

Sir Arthur Currie

SOUVENIRS OF VICTORY

As a sign of victory, Canadian soldiers collected souvenirs of the battlefield. The most prized possessions were German helmets, Luger pistols and Iron Cross medals (awarded for gallantry).

This Iron Cross was taken by Private Edwin Taylor of Sackville, New Brunswick, who served with the 26th Canadian Infantry Battalion and survived the war with a gunshot wound to the right thigh.

Iron Cross, 2nd Class

"Any man who ... said he was never scared is just pretty hard to believe ... but it is entirely a matter of controlling that fear."

Lance Corporal Gordon Hamilton,
58th Canadian Infantry Battalion

"I look back on our advance through machine gun and shell fire over open country and I feel that nothing but the power of prayer ever saved me."

Lieutenant Horatio Cromwell,
38th Canadian Infantry Battalion

"Damn this dirty, lousy, stinking bloody war."

Private George Bell,
1st Canadian Infantry Battalion

"My friend was killed in the last push which makes it pretty lonesome for me.... You never know what minute you are a dead man here. Shells burst around you that would blow up a building the size of a house."

Private Earl Bolton,
Canadian Machine Gun Corps

"The whole front was one mass of smoke, dust and flames. How anything or anyone could live through it, I do not know."

Lieutenant Warren Hendershot,
Royal Flying Corps

CAMBRAI

THE BATTLE FOR CAMBRAI — SEPTEMBER 27 TO OCTOBER 9, 1918

The Great Powers of Europe had all absorbed crippling casualties during the course of the war. Under the onslaught, Germany's allies, Turkey and Austria–Hungary, were wavering badly and on the verge of surrender. Germany, too, was close to seeking an armistice, but still its soldiers fought on.

On the Canadian front, the Canal du Nord was the last major obstacle preventing the Allies from reaching Cambrai, the enemy's key rail and road junction in northern France.

The Canadian Corps had triumphed at Amiens and Arras, but had lost close to 25,000 soldiers. Sir Arthur Currie believed his soldiers had one last great battle in them. This would be another combined arms operation, with all units working together to defeat the Germans, who had the significant advantage of fighting from prepared trenches and strongpoints.

CROSSING THE CANAL — SEPTEMBER 27, 1918

Under cover of heavy artillery and machine-gun fire, the Canadians attacked at 5:20 a.m. on September 27. The infantry surged across the canal, overcoming German resistance. Behind the lead waves of infantry, engineers facing enemy fire hastily constructed the bridges needed to move guns, supplies and vehicles over the banks.

The Canadian infantry and machine gunners fought their way forward, capturing the strongpoint of Bourlon Wood, and then pushed eastward to allow more forces to follow them as they drove toward Cambrai.

But the Germans would not give up their critical logistical city without a fight.

"I would prefer to go without Infantry rather than without Engineers."

Sir Arthur Currie

 Captain Roberts' Uniform

CANADIAN ENGINEERS

Canadian engineers played a key role in the combined arms battles of the Hundred Days.

By 1918, the Canadian Corps had developed a robust engineering capacity to support the infantry. Twelve engineering battalions built roads and bridges, found water supplies and cleared enemy-laid explosives. The attack at Canal du Nord could not have succeeded without the bridges that allowed artillery and tanks to cross the divide.

This is the uniform of Captain Frederick Roberts, who served with the 3rd Battalion Canadian Engineers from August 1916. Throughout the Hundred Days campaign, he commanded a company of sappers who were involved in road repair, bridge building, deactivating hidden explosives and active combat. Roberts survived the war.

"This isn't war, it's murder. It's just pure bloody murder."

Lieutenant Joseph Sproston,
10th Canadian Infantry Battalion

IT SEEMED IMPOSSIBLE — SEPTEMBER 28 TO OCTOBER 9, 1918

Recovering from the assault, the Germans threw everything they had against the Canadians. It was not enough.

In brutal fighting from September 28, one by one the enemy positions fell, with the Canadians overrunning the enemy defences. "Never have I felt so depressed as I felt after that battle," wrote the 7th Brigade's Brigadier J. A. Clark. "It seemed impossible to break the morale and fighting spirit of the German troops." But the weary Canadians pressed on in the final battle for Cambrai.

VICKERS MACHINE GUN

The British Vickers machine gun was most deadly in a defensive role. In the fighting around Cambrai, machine guns like this one, operated by a team of three gunners, cut down the German soldiers as they repeatedly counterattacked the Canadians. The Vickers provided crucial firepower for the Canadian infantry who were exhausted and often outnumbered.

THE CHEMICAL BATTLEFIELD

The German and Allied armies saturated the front with poison gas during the 1918 battles. Phosgene and mustard gas could lead to suffocation, fluid-filled lungs, damaged eyes and scorched skin.

Soldiers needed respirators to survive. While respirators like this one were effective in filtering out the gas, wearing them left soldiers fatigued and frightened within the swirling death clouds.

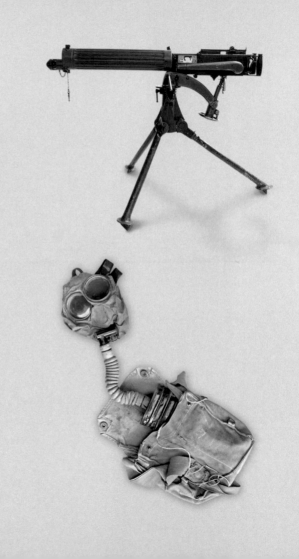

**Vickers
Mk. 1
Machine Gun**

**Small Box
Respirator**

JOHN MacGREGOR, V.C.

A fearless soldier and a born leader, Captain John MacGregor served first as a private in the 2nd Canadian Mounted Rifles and later as an officer. He was one of Canada's most decorated soldiers.

MacGregor earned the Victoria Cross for his courage during the fierce battles to the west of Cambrai between September 29 and October 3.

Lieutenant-Colonel MacGregor's Medal Set

1. Victoria Cross
2. Military Cross With Bar
3. Distinguished Conduct Medal
4. 1914–15 Star
5. British War Medal 1914–1920
6. Victory Medal 1914–1919
7. 1939–45 Star
8. Canadian Volunteer Service Medal With Overseas Bar
9. War Medal 1939–1945
10. King George VI Coronation Medal 1937
11. Canadian Efficiency Decoration

In one clash, he singlehandedly attacked a series of machine guns, killing four Germans and capturing eight prisoners. MacGregor survived the war and died in Powell River, British Columbia, on June 9, 1952.

SEIZING CAMBRAI

With its important road and rail junction, Cambrai was the main enemy supply centre in northern France. Liberating the city would cripple the Germans, and the Canadian attack in the early hours of October 9 caught them by surprise.

Entering the city, the Canadians discovered that the enemy had evacuated much of the population, looted everything and set many buildings on fire. Canadian engineers put out the flames, and Cambrai was saved.

The German high command, now unable to supply its forces at the front, ordered a general retreat.

Canadians Entering Cambrai

Lithograph made by Frank Brangwyn in 1918

THE AFTERMATH OF BATTLE

The capture of Cambrai broke the Germans' defensive system and sent them into retreat. It was a decisive victory for the battle-weary Canadians.

Though Currie considered the attack at the Canal du Nord his greatest victory, his worn-out troops had suffered heavily in the almost continuous battles.

The Germans ordered 11 divisions to hold Cambrai and failed. The four divisions of the Canadian Corps had soundly defeated the enemy, but at the heavy cost of 13,620 men killed, wounded or captured.

**Lance Corporal
Eby's Medal Set**

1. British War Medal
   1914–1920

2. Victory Medal
   1914–1919

**Memorial
Plaque**

ELGIN EBY

Lance Corporal Elgin Eby of the 75th Canadian Infantry Battalion was one of several thousand Canadians killed in the many battles to capture Cambrai. Pre-war, he was a skilled labourer living in Berlin, Ontario. The city's name was changed to Kitchener during the war because of anti-German sentiment.

Eby was killed in combat on September 30, 1918, at age 23. Following Eby's death in battle, his next of kin received this memorial plaque and his medals. Tens of thousands of plaques like this one were issued to grieving families across Canada.

"It made one feel that all this fighting had been worthwhile to see a people so glad to be delivered from hard rulers."

Private William Davidson,
72nd Battery, Canadian Field Artillery

MONS

THE MARCH TO MONS

Germany and its allies — under the relentless strain of four long years of war and millions of deaths — had reached the point of collapse.

And still the enemy fought on, although close to surrender and in full retreat. The German Army had been decisively defeated in battle after battle during the Hundred Days.

This print by British artist Paul Nash captures the Canadians' march along a seemingly never-ending road in pursuit of the Germans.

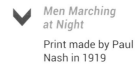

Men Marching at Night

Print made by Paul Nash in 1919

LIBERATION

With the Germans retreating, the Canadians liberated dozens of French and Belgian towns and cities. They were greeted with relief and gratitude by thousands of civilians who had suffered under German occupation for over four years.

Setting people free from tyranny, many Canadian soldiers felt that their terrible sacrifices during the war had been worthwhile. But at the same time, listening to the civilians' stories of looting, destruction, repression and executions under German occupation served to intensify the anger Canadians felt toward the enemy.

THE FINAL BATTLE — VALENCIENNES, OCTOBER 31 TO NOVEMBER 2, 1918

Valenciennes, securely held by German defenders who had made a stand there after their long retreat, was the site of the last Canadian set-piece battle.

Sir Arthur Currie's plan was to use a massive deluge of shells against the Germans on Mont Houy, the hill at the heart of the enemy defences. The extraordinary bombardment fired by hundreds of guns stunned and shattered two enemy divisions. Canadian infantry surged forward and the Germans were forced into retreat again.

Grateful French citizens in Valenciennes welcomed their Canadian liberators with this handmade Red Ensign, Canada's wartime flag. This Red Ensign and a French flag were the first flags displayed in the Valenciennes city hall at the end of the German occupation.

Red Ensign

7th. 8th. 9th C.I.Bdes.   C.R.A.   C.R.E.   D.M.G.C.   Signals
A.D.M.S.   A.&.Q.   Divl.Train.   A.P.M.   Camp Comdt.
A.D.C for G.O.C.

G.328   11

Hostilities will cease at 1100 hours on Nov.11th AAA   Troops

will stand fast on the line reached at that hour which will be

reported to ~~Camps~~ *DIVL.* H.Q.   AAA   Defensive precautions will be

maintained   AAA   There will be no intercourse of any

description with the enemy AAA   Further instructions follow

AAA   9th Cdn.Inf.Bde will take over front from 7th Cdn.Inf.

Bde. as soon as possible AAA   Arrangements direct between

Brigades.   AAA   Adsd.List 'A'

   From - 3rd Cdn.Divn.
          0810

                                                    Major G.S.

CAPTURING MONS

The British high command ordered Currie to capture Mons on November 10. Taking the historic Belgian city, where the British first fought the Germans in August 1914, would be the crowning achievement in the Hundred Days campaign.

Front-line soldiers complained that they did not want to attack Mons. Each feared being the last man to die. But no one was certain the war would really end, so the Canadians prepared for the assault.

As the Canadians captured Mons in the early hours of November 11, Currie's headquarters was informed by army command that the war would end at 11 a.m. on November 11, 1918. The 3rd Canadian Infantry Division sent this telegram to its units early in the morning. Similar telegrams and messages were passed throughout the Canadian Corps. Soldiers at the front were ordered to dig deep and to take no chances.

◀ Cessation of Hostilities Telegram

THE LAST SOLDIER KILLED

Private George Price, age 25, from Port Williams, Nova Scotia, served with the 28th Canadian Infantry Battalion.

While most Canadians took cover in the final hours of the war, Price led a patrol northeast of Mons. A German sniper shot him minutes before the Armistice on November 11, 1918. Private Price was the last Canadian and Commonwealth soldier killed in battle on the Western Front.

"Wouldn't it be Hell to be knocked off the last day?"

**Lieutenant W. A. Dunlop,
116th Canadian Infantry Battalion**

Private Price's Medal Set

1. British War Medal 1914–1920
2. Victory Medal 1914–1919

"We had left behind the comradeship of long hours on trench post and patrols ... and we were entering a cold sea, facing the dark, the unknown we could not escape."

Private Will Bird,
42nd Canadian Infantry Battalion

RETURN TO CANADA

VICTORY AND SACRIFICE

The Allied forces defeated the German Army in battle during the Hundred Days campaign. An Armistice ended the war on November 11, 1918.

Two Canadian divisions formed part of the Allied forces responsible for the occupation of Germany. With more than 45,000 casualties suffered in the Hundred Days campaign, the Canadians were weary and angry. They expected to face a hostile civilian population, but the Germans had no more fight in them.

The Canadian citizen-soldiers desperately wanted to go home and were increasingly frustrated by the slow process of repatriation. Riots and disturbances broke out in the months following the Armistice. These incidents frightened the British authorities into fast-tracking the Canadians' departure, with most soldiers returning to their communities and families by the summer of 1919.

SHOCK TROOPS FORGOTTEN

The Canadian Corps was a dependable, hard-hitting spearhead formation that delivered victory throughout the Hundred Days campaign

In battle after battle, the Canadian Corps defeated the Germans, using their combined arms approach to warfare. This major contribution to the Allies' victory far outweighed the Canadian Corps' relative size and strength. But weapon systems and tactics alone do not win wars. Victory was due to thousands of soldiers fighting together with their comrades and drawing on a deep well of courage and tenacity.

Despite the elite reputation the Canadian soldiers had earned overseas, the memory of their victories in 1918 rapidly faded once the soldiers had returned home.

*Lieutenant General
Sir Arthur Currie,
GCMG, KCB*

Painted by Sir William
Orpen in 1919

A GENERAL CONDEMNED

Lieutenant-General Sir Arthur Currie was one of the Allies' finest generals. But in Canada, and even among his own soldiers, there was anger over the extent of casualties suffered during the Hundred Days campaign.

In March 1919, the belligerent former minister of militia and defence Sam Hughes accused Currie of being a butcher, particularly in his ordering of the Mons attack. These shocking and unfounded charges meant Currie returned to a cold welcome in August 1919, and left him feeling betrayed by his government.

In June 1927, a newspaper in Port Hope, Ontario, printed Hughes' charges. Currie, by then the principal of McGill University in Montréal, sued the newspaper for libel.

From March to April 1928, the courtroom cross-examination scrutinized — and ridiculed — Currie's wartime decisions. Canadians followed the sensational trial closely. Currie was vindicated when he eventually won the case.

The strain of the trial shattered Currie. He suffered a stroke from which he never fully recovered and died at age 58 on November 30, 1933.

THE DEAD AND THE SURVIVORS

More than 9 million soldiers died during the First World War and millions more were wounded, in body and spirit. Countless civilians perished.

Canada paid a terrible price. More than 61,000 men and women died during the war, thousands more in its aftermath, and 173,000 suffered wounds, many permanently disabled. The country reeled from the losses.

Almost all of Canada's wartime dead remain buried overseas in Commonwealth War Graves Commission cemeteries. The survivors returned home and tried to move on with their lives.

The war receded into the past, but it was never forgotten. Canadians have spent a century grappling with the sacrifices that forever changed their nation.

CONTRIBUTIONS

This souvenir catalogue reflects the contributions of the many people who made the exhibition possible. Special exhibitions like this are a collective undertaking by the entire staff of the Canadian War Museum. The core exhibition team received support from the Collections, Corporate Affairs, Exhibitions and Research divisions, along with many colleagues from the Canadian Museum of History. We would like to acknowledge the individuals and institutions that loaned artifacts, supplied images and directed us to important sources, enriching the exhibition and this catalogue. Special thanks go to the National Film Board and the Vimy Foundation.

The core team consisted of project manager Kirby Sayant, creative development specialist Marie-Louise Deruaz, collections specialist Eric Fernberg, learning specialist Sandra O'Quinn, communications manager Avra Gibbs Lamey, and the two author-curators of this catalogue. The team appreciates support from senior managers Kathryn Lyons, Dr. Peter MacLeod, Glenn Ogden, James Whitham and Caroline Dromaguet. Additional thanks to photographers Bill Kent and Susan Ross, to contract historian Colin Garnett and to Lee Wyndham, who oversaw the production of this catalogue.

DONOR RECOGNITION

GENEROUSLY SUPPORTED BY
John and Elizabeth Irving

WITH ADDITIONAL SUPPORT FROM
Dr. John Scott Cowan and the Sir Joseph Flavelle Foundation

OFFICIAL PARTNERS, FIRST WORLD WAR CENTENARY

R. Howard Webster Foundation
Fondation R. Howard Webster

John and Pattie Cleghorn and Family

HCol (Ret'd) John C. Eaton, O.Ont., K.St.J., D.Com. and HCol (Ret'd) Sally Horsfall Eaton, S.S.St.J., C.D., R.N., LL.D.

PHOTO CREDITS

Canadian War Museum

p. 5	IMG2012-0213-005-Dp1 / Photo: Steven Darby
p. 6	19930012-419
p. 9	19930012-342
p. 10	19930012-760
p. 16	George Metcalf Archival Collection / 20000013-017
p. 18	George Metcalf Archival Collection / 19820602-011
p. 20	19801226-013, 051, 040
p. 23	George Metcalf Archival Collection / 19930012-791
p. 24	George Metcalf Archival Collection / 19700140-061c
p. 27	19390001-079
p. 28	19820169-001
p. 30	George Metcalf Archival Collection / 19930012-63
p. 32	19880212-093
p. 34	19440017-001
p. 37	(top) Tilston Memorial Collection of Canadian Military Medals / 20130405-001
p. 37	(bottom) George Metcalf Archival Collection / 19940079-032
p. 39	Tilston Memorial Collection of Canadian Military Medals / 20080037-001
p. 40	19390002-229
p. 42	George Metcalf Archival Collection / 19930012-427
p. 45	George Metcalf Archival Collection / 19930012-528
p. 46	19820498-002
p. 47	George Metcalf Archival Collection / 19940003-905
p. 50	19930012-635
p. 53	(top) 20130349-006
p. 53	(bottom) 20130349-004
p. 55	20070067-234
p. 57	Beaverbrook Collection of War Art / 19710261-0057
p. 58	(bottom) 19390002-108
p. 60	Beaverbrook Collection of War Art / 19710261-0749
p. 63	Beaverbrook Collection of War Art / 19710261-0434
p. 64	George Metcalf Archival Collection / 19880001-836

External Sources